DANCING INSIDE THE MOUTH OF MADNESS

New poems

Michael N. Thompson

Nine Twenty Two Publishing
Los Angeles

Dancing Inside the Mouth of Madness

Copyright © 2008 by Michael N. Thompson

ISBN: 978-0-6151-9127-0

Front cover photo and inset photo by Christina DeMasi
Back cover photo by Michael N. Thompson

Email: miketro1@yahoo.com
Website: www.myspace.com/hollywoodpoet
Rants: http://poetincalifornia.blogspot.com

CONTENTS

ACKNOWLEDGEMENTS

Very special thanks to Christina and the rest of the DeMasi family for supporting me and taking me in as one of their own. Thank you seems to be far too insignificant to say, but I'll say it anyway and I love all of you very much especially my very significant other.

Other thanks go to Scott (Cardinals! Cardinals!) Karla (I bet a steak would hit the spot)) Kristina (Yes I know you are a bitch, but I love you anyway) Becky (how could you name your dog after my cat?) Cindy (as in photo credit by...) Larvell (what will be done first, your "Novella" or Brian Griffin's so called novel?) Jamaal (stop stalking Kim Kardashian's SUV) and the rest of you that I am fortunate to call my friends for putting up with my antics over the years. No you are not getting a free copy. Don't be so tight. You all have jobs.

Big hugs go out to Warren Fulton, Lisa Powell, Grey Anderson and Beth Jannery for the kind words and helpful advice.

A special no thanks goes out to the certain (OK most) members of my family. You know what you did and why I have such contempt for you.

Thanks Mom. Thanks Dad. For absolutely nothing.

I would also like to congratulate myself for not losing my mind during the writing of these poems, though I had plenty of opportunities to do so.

The poem "Story of My Life" was previously published by Pooka Press as part of their Photo Booth Broadside Series.

NINE MONTHS IN THE WOMB WAS MEANINGLESS

I cannot forgive your faithlessness
A boy says to his mother
You can hang my picture
In the gallery
Next to your bedroom door
But it won't change a thing
Someday when I grow into a man
I will still carry the grief
Of a fire that's been extinguished
And you will try
To relight the flame
But my veins
Will be filled with water

I asked no quarter
And none was given
Even when I was devoured
By the barbed wire of emotion
Like the day
He began to whip me
With a tree branch
In front of my friends
I hoped he would whip me to death
So I wouldn't have to face them in shame
But of course he didn't
And I couldn't look at them
In the eye for days
Bearing the scars of the beatings
From a man who wasn't my father
While YOU mother stood silent
This spoke louder than war to me
Did you hear my cries
Echoing in the hallway?
How could you just look away?

The only friend I had
Was my dog Poppy
Who would try valiantly to protect me
From the hand of a man
That only knew violence and yelling
Until the day I felt so non existent
That I rose up and bit
The hand that bleeds

It's been a thousand years
Since I woke up in California
Cast aside like some broken toy
You think you know
Everything that I am
But you don't know me at all
How many times
Did I break into your car
Just so I'd have shelter
From the cruel night
Mother your pieces break off
A little more
As each autumn passes
I'm tired of holding my breath
Hoping you'd change your mind
Or at the very least change sides
But I guess those nine months
In the womb were meaningless

GHOSTS

Craving the dying ghosts
From incest's temple
Martyred by the thorn
That bleeds me
The molding crust
Of yesterday
Is lodged
In my throat
And I engage
In a multiplicity
Of different masks
Each one to fit
The role I played
Memories of empty days
Have fallen to pieces
Under the weight
Of the undertow
Veins are filled
With the tusks
Of invisible ghosts
Punching through the walls
Of a paper cup
Caked with the barbs
And frayed
Like a live wire
I hollow myself
In jukebox bars
Until the bed of nails
That I bleed on
Is cold and rusted
While dust gathers
On the shelf
Where my picture
Used to sit
Another ghost in the machine

KISS OF LIFE

I was the boy
That couldn't swim
Left to drown
In the deep end
Of the gene pool
The room I used to live in
Is nothing but books and dust now
Walls still breathe
And penetrate like a vice
As a reel of home movies
Plays in my head
Pieces of me
Left in a pile of maple leaves
So easily replaced
And easily forgotten
The silence of abandonment
Screams like a siren
Through twisted bones
Until I'm ashes
Though the open fields
In the empty spaces
Of my head
Is my favorite place to be
In the silence and the shadows
Skin is merely stitches
And I'm still waiting
For the kiss of life

VODKA AND ORANGE JUICE

Living this Dylan Thomas life
With the viciousness of a lion
The carnival of scars
Built from a summer in Yosemite
When I was plied with vodka and orange juice
Until I was incapacitated
So I've placed my shame in a box
That I open up every now and then
Just to see if it still exists
As I've walked for miles
From Westchester to Brentwood
Just to find something
Or someone to be
Through jaded eyes I frown
As the dirty streets I roam
Crack like leaves underneath my feet
And I blood let until I'm numb

CUTTER

Carving words like blood
Wound into fragile skin
Is the only way to find shelter
From the damage
Nobody saw the crying
The razors or the scars
Nor the empty rooms
Filled with cheap wine
As rape bleeds from open veins
The vortex of wasted years
Lashes across my heart
Christmas seems colorless
While shades of abortion
Infect me like cancer
That's what happens
When you walk through existence
So fucking blatantly unwanted
I cut myself
When bliss is but a ghost
And the disarray
Is just a reminder
That affliction is never too far away

HELICOPTER

Soaked with wine
And memories
Of better days
The halo of scars
That veils a martyr
Thick with alchemy
Like a viper
Leaves me drowning
In the killing fields
Of rape and exile
Where a porcelain heart
Pierced by cruelties
By thorns that devour
Falls from a whisper
To a scream
Like the blades
Of a helicopter

POSTCARDS FROM THE EDGE

Bleeding from a cardboard box
Breath is filled with dirt
Surrounded by the four walls of torment
Until swollen beyond repair
Hiding from my disgrace
In the company of my mistress
I tear myself to shreds
For I'll never know
The beauty of romance
Since I've cocooned
My fragile heart
And veiled this life
Behind the mask of illusion
While I watch my words
Drip onto the page
Until a soul
Is there for all to see
Fading away
In a cheap motel
Along the boulevard
I'm not going home
Instead I'm sending postcards
From the edge of dislocation

HOUSE OF PAIN

Blood means nothing
In the house of pain
As spiders fall
From mother's lips
And madness coats
The walls of this prison
The way cheap wine
Coats my belly
Swollen like ashen dragonflies
And languishing inside this asylum
Until the soul atrophies
Into a bleeding shell
As the beetles
And spires of morphed
Drench in a thick coat
Of invisibility
While memories peel
Like photographs
Sleeping in the sun
All I am is remains
Of strangers and monsters
While a naked heart
Twists and numbs
As the house of pain
Fills with ashes

STORY OF MY LIFE

The story of my life
Is a diary
Filled with chapters
Of lies and regret
I created everything
From pages and denial
As the wreckage
Of my past implodes
But I brought this
All upon myself
Sometimes I try
And forget to breathe
Just for the drama
And the sympathy
Pictures left
In a shoebox
That no one sees
Rot and mold
Until much like
The life I've lived
The photos are colorless

EVERGREEN

Slipping beneath
The surface of life
After crawling out
From the wreckage
Of a wished abortion
And cast aside
Like paper flowers
Carrying the damage
As a crucible
While nerve ends drip
With scars and violence
And redemption
Lays in pieces
Like a broken doll
Until the complete absence
Of credible souvenirs
Leaves me craving
For a moment
Of evergreen

PERMANENT INK

The sheep of this town seem to have made it in vogue to stain their bodies in one way or another, but unlike their blatant and futile attempts to be part of the "in" crowd, my reasons are much more ethereal. I have marked my skin with the needle's ink because I wear each tattoo as a scar that tells a story of whom I am and where I've been. My flesh is drenched in tattoos for nothing more than they read like the chapters of my life. Call it permanent ink, if you will. The anarchy symbol is to remind me of the chaos and madness I overcame not to become either one of my parents. The logo of my favorite band adorns my body in remembrance of an innocence lost from days gone by when the end of summer days was the closest thing I could get to a tragedy. The stamp of the Latin phrase "Carpe Diem" is tattooed on me as a statement that no matter what tomorrow might bring (and despite the blunt force trauma brought to my head and my heart by so called loved ones) that I still live for the moment. The Japanese symbols for "Poem" and "Redemption" line the inside of my arm for vindication towards the ones that have betrayed. I've recreated past days in the words of my poems instead of pouring out my heart in front of a shrink the way a bartender pours out drinks at a downtown bar. The words "Made in California" line the inside of my other arm to show pride in where I come from. Every time I look at those words on my skin, I think of the streets of San Francisco where I was introduced to this world and how disconnected I felt when I left my first home. Perhaps it's why I long to return there. Maybe I just crave to be full circle. The bat winged viper in hooker/stripper attire pretty much summarizes how I feel about women in general. I guess I'm looking for a woman that's sexy and dangerous, but yet will submit to me in the bedroom. The again, I can be a bit of a paradox since I also seem to have a fetish for the bookish type. You know the type that puts her hair up and hides behind black rimmed glasses. The kind with an outward appearance of a good girl, but that's the opposite of who she really is. If the eyes are the window to the soul, then the ink that marks my skin is the graffiti that colors the walls.

DISASSOCIATION

The flesh and bone
Of those that pierced
Instead of embracing
Would be cold as winter
If you weren't so numb
The disassociation
Of what should be sacred
Echoes and lingers
Until obsession
Is the drug
In the house of affliction
And you're crushed
By the leaves
Of loneliness
Until the company
Of strangers
Feels like home
Wake up screaming
In a bed of fire
And the room
In the basement
So you're out of the way
And unseen
As it somewhat resembles
A prison
It convinces you
That not being there
Would be better
For everyone involved
And it isn't long
Before they agree
And you're riding
The steel wheels
Of a Greyhound bus
To California
Where you decide
This can't get any worse

I WON'T DIE FROM THIS

The sting whips
Against naïve skin
Until I feel
More loathsome
Than handsome
While karma
Gags and binds
Now my plate is clean
As regret dances
In mocking fashion
And faith falls
Like thorns
From broken flowers
And the sad song nights
Of being sold
Down the river
Like a slave
Have concluded
Since I'm learning
To live again
And I discovered
That I won't die from this

OVERWHELMED

Summer ended
When the flowers faded
And pedals
Became ashes
Turning the page
To better days
And memories
Until miles
From the rejection
It's taken
A decade or two
To release the hurting
From my lips
Now there's nothing left
But regrets and stains
From the years
That passed by slowly
Without words
Or apologies
I can't say
That I'll be there
On heaven's highest hill
When the music's over
As the road I chose
Wasn't always
Straight and narrow
But this will remain
Like a photograph
And I swear
I won't be
Overwhelmed again

BLINK

In the time it takes to blink
I was pulled down by the undertow
And I've been fighting
To keep my head above water ever since
There are no memories of family picnics
No dinner table conversations
Of "how was school today?"
No nights of gathering around the television
To watch Happy Days or the Mary Tyler Moore Show
There is only emptiness and bitter salty tears
There are no vacation slides
From when we went to the Grand Canyon
Or black and white photos
From the year we went to Disneyland
No funny stories of when we went camping
And it rained the whole time we were there
There's nothing but the craven hollow

DAMAGED GOODS

The cycle of pain
And damage done
Turn to scabs
That will never heal
And the phantoms
That swallows me whole
Until I'm stripped naked
Bleed me like a viper
Or a scarred slave atrophied
While bruises burn
Skin and bones
Angels leave me
For those less tormented
As I dance
With the devil inside
Fragile from the numb
And breaking into
A million pieces
That leads to treachery
Behind the serpent's mask
Wounds the bastard son
And dragon's wings
Binds me in tethers
Until I'm used
Like a punching bag
And I'm nothing more
Than damaged goods

GREY

Dancing with the dying flowers
Of dementia and lucidity
In a prison
Where even angels
Fear to tread
The isolation of silence
A mother's gift
To a son
Whispers its existence
In slow motion
Where inside the beautiful house
Of delusion and denial
Yesterday's heroes
Bleed like butterflies
As imitation colors
Turn to grey
And these phantoms sleep
On this bed of nails
Here with me
While I blood let
From the dysfunction
And I wear this crown
To keep the ice from melting
It takes more
Than a tourniquet
When you're living
In the grey

DISCONNECTED

Standing on the edge
Of a bare existence
In the straightjacket
Of desolation
Where the cycle
Of tragedy
Breeds like flies
Until I'm disconnected
From the influence
Of my bloodline
And the sting
Digs sharper and deeper
Than barbed wire
While the blade
Drags my soul
Through fields of thorns
Until I'm disconnected
From the world
That's disconnected me

SCARS

In the coma
Of this existence
Torment bleaches my bones
Until the scars estrange
And drown me
In a sea
Of self loathing
Where they remind me
Of the crash
And the beauty
Of when yesterday
Collided with innocence
I'm tired
Of stitching myself
Wouldn't it be better
If the tattooed girls
Brought their own
Needle and thread
If every scar
Tells a story
Deep cuts
The knife indeed

LAST TRAIN HOME

Falling like cigarette ashes
Ink breathes from living scars
While another wine soaked year passes
But I'll bear this cross
Until it splinters
As the silent affliction of torment
Stains with slings and arrows
Though I flounder in self doubt
And states of confusion
Strangles violently
By the talons of madness
Left with a crumpled heart
And empty pockets
It's hard to confront a wooden box
Buried six feet in the ground
When you're tainted
Made of thorns
Stripped to wire and ashes
Inhaling the damage done
And left to die in California
Stung by the tragedy
Like chlorine in an open wound
Until I'm naked as a martyr
As stardust clings to bleeding ink
While the last train home
Leaves the station without me
I ask myself
How long before I'm numb
To all of this

COMA

Bleed my eyes
With the thorns
Of disillusion
Numb and blistered
Martyred by the roots
From the dirt
Filled with regret
And suffering through
The human drama
That chokes to death
But scars have no conscience
Nor does the whiplash kiss
The shape of my heart
Has begun to crumble
Under the weight
Of this torment
And the memories
Twist and distort
As I fade
Into an emotional coma

MAYBE IT WAS JUST MY BOYISH CHARM

Too many years were wasted on fucking anonymous women just so I could fill the void of emptiness that bleached my bones. I seemed to have an uncanny knack for attracting the vulnerable and tormented bursting with tragedy. It really all started with Missy Leno who was a classic case of engaging in promiscuity with a series of older men in a futile attempt to replace an absent father. While my experience with her was completely forgettable, it started a pattern of romances with affection starved moths looking for the flame of love. What they failed to realize was that I was so tormented by the tragedy bestowed on me by the family tree, that the religion of lust was all that I believed in. Its amusing the clarity I have years later to notice what I couldn't see back then. Between the strippers that screamed for attention that was non existent in their word of denial, the bored and unfaithful housewives that left a trail in my bed when they'd sober up and realized that the man they sleep next to didn't turn them on anymore and the young girls who's fathers had long since abandoned them without a trace, my dance card was kept full though I was just a temporary fix. As soon as they'd yearn for something more permanent, I'd take a new train to the next girl.

STIGMATA

Naked and fragile
As the dust of angels
Bleeds with self affliction
Spiraling into darkness
Until it hurts to exist
Dancing in the screams
Of suffocation
And burdened by the colors
Of bitterness
And tainted by the religion
Of lies
While I crawl across
The cracked existence
Of my torment
Filled with revolution
And razor blades
Misery and depression pills
With the wounds of Christ
Tattooed on my back

FOLD

Lost inside
A world of fear
Where the darkest
Part of me
Is infected
With suffocation
Close to the edge
Of confusion
And dementia
A heart soaked
With disillusion
Entangled in madness
Laying face down
In fields of fire
Drowning in the abyss
Of the beautiful soil
Bleeding and craving
The slave in me surfaces
And breaks me down
Until I fold

LESS THAN ZERO

Bleeding like abortion
In a Thunderbird coma
While the ghosts of yesterday
Coat me with static
Until I'm bludgeoned
By the talons of disregard
And naked
As a crucified beetle
In the cage made for me
The regret binds
And drenches
In the calligraphy
Of torment
With each graceless day
Of a flood filled existence
Fractured recollections
Buried in a shoebox
Beneath the soil
From the garden
Leaves blood on their hands
And I'm dying
For the bone collector
As I lay tethered
From the riptide
Becoming less than zero

VALIDATION

Still dying for validation
After all these years
A borderline obsession
Since my old man
Left me far behind
For a life of anonymity
Sometimes I felt
Like a social pariah
And other times
Just merely invisible
High school was tempestuous
Because of the battlefield
That I called home
But I made it out
Of the halls alive
And when I stood there
In that cap and gown
The best I got
Was not an ounce of pride
But complete surprise
That I could do it
In the first place
As those
That brought this decay
Echo inside of me
And are the reasons why
I put my words
On the page
And with each life
That passes by
Clouds crash like thunder
Under a darkened sky
Its no wonder
That I'm jaded

SPIRES

Curls of barbed wire
Wrap around
This naked heart
And the ugliness
Of self destruction
Looks beautiful to me
In the delirious darkness
Of a prison
Made of flesh and bone
There's no room left
In this faithless heart
As breakdowns
Fill my head
With its twisted blade
And tormented memories
Nailed to the blood
Of my wounds
As I untangle the threads
Of misplaced emotion
Bound on cathedral spires

DUST

Dancing in killing fields
Of thorns and azure
Where the leaves
Are made of glass
And regret
As gardens of ashes
Fill eyes with lust
The bed I sleep in
Is numb and gray
Leaves me feeling
Like a photograph
Lying on an empty shelf
Morphine lips
Grind into sand
Until I scream
And I'm covered
In my cocoon
Naked in my dust

THE FILM IN MY HEAD

Breathing in fear and flowers
The salvation of madness
Seems like nirvana
Compared to this
And I find myself
Standing on the pavement
Outside the house
On eighth avenue
Where I grew wings
And had to go
From 12 to 20
Seemingly overnight
As I lost myself
To damaged girls
Bound to the tether
Of self destruction
Just so I could disappear
Regrets sting more
In an empty room
Through the windows
And against the walls
The film in my head
Plays a drama
Of kaleidoscope memories
From days gone by

PHOTOGRAPHS

Pictures of her oldest son
Hanging on the wall
The fear and emptiness
That has hollowed
For all these years
From being
A regretful mistake
And swept
Under the carpet
Goes unnoticed
Does she just
Close her eyes
And bathe
In the denial
Until regret lingers
Like a phantom
In the heart
While long forgotten photographs
Put away on
A dusty shelf
Always rear
Their ugly head
When you don't
Want them to

CLOSURE

Beyond fragile husks
Of better days
And beneath
The ashen remains
Of a former prodigal son
I thank God
That denial
Isn't hereditary
The beetles
That used to sting
Have been crushed
And left for dead
The way I used to be
The angel of desolation
Doesn't sleep in my bed
As often as she used to
And I wouldn't miss her
If she didn't knock
At my door again
Maybe I've grown up
Or just grown so cold
That nothing matters anymore
I don't need closure
To breathe again

NOT QUITE HOME FOR THE HOLIDAYS

There's nothing like the holidays to make you feel invisible. Unless you've walked down streets emptier than the hollow shell of your soul, then you probably don't know what I mean. Have you ever looked through the windows of houses where families are gathered around a dining room table as they bask in the moment of being all together? Have you ever completely non existent because that is something you will never taste? Dear reader, I have a lifetime of these paper memories. I could tell you about the time that I wandered through the snow laden sidewalks of the town I lived in at the time, just looking for a bar to numb myself so I wouldn't have to be reminded that the rest of my so called family was celebrating another Thanksgiving without me in the picture. I remember one year when I returned to the town I grew up in for New Year's and ended up sneaking into my stepfather's tool shed so I had somewhere dry to sleep. I looked up at the second floor where the lights lit up the family room and I listened to them (and various neighbors that had dropped by) laugh and drink in the New Year. As for me, I ended up wrapping myself into a ball and shivered relentlessly until I was too drained to stay awake any longer. Then there was that one Christmas that I spent in a motel room so I wouldn't be home alone when everyone I knew was with someone exchanging gifts. Or the year I spent Christmas morning just sitting on the pier in Santa Monica hoping that someone else would come along so that at least I wouldn't be the only one in a out there, but no one ever appeared. I just ended up spending the day with the seagulls instead. I haven't even mentioned the countless holidays spent in a tiny apartment drinking cheap wine just in the hopes that I'd pass out so the day would go by faster. You'd think that since I'm with a girl that loves me and takes me every year to spend Christmas with her family, all of this would bleed away. You would think that dear reader, but you'd be mistaken. Being there in a room full of people that I only see once a year just reminds me that I'm not part of them and all I end up feeling is claustrophobic.

EASIER TO EXILE

It was just easier
To exile me
Than to live with me
And the years
Of being bastardized
Has frozen me
To the point
Of indifference
And their mentality
Of "what will the neighbors think"
Until in a plot twist
The tables turned
Into an ironic rhythm
Of being offended
That I turned my back
On birthdays
And personal milestones
I've heard that karma
Is a bitch
It looks to me
Like the bitch is back

WIDE AWAKE AND DEAD

Invisible inside
The bell jar
Of Sylvia Path
And saturated
In brilliant crucifixion
From the black veil
Of dysfunction
As the dragon's belly
Fills my mouth
With ashes
And the baptism
Of the undertow
Martyrs me
Until I'm knee deep
In the schizophrenia
That binds
Like a tourniquet
And stings like beetles
While I blood let
Behind a scar filled mask
And build
A house of cards
As a shield

PEDESTRIAN

Living on candy bars
Soda pop and potato chips
The years spent
In down at the mouth
Bars and rooming houses
While seemingly tragic
At the time
Formed the words
In my head
Until I was ready
To write them down
While I wandered
The canyons and gutters
As a bohemian
Bleeding romanticize
And the emotional instability
Of barstool junkies
That bled
In and out
Of my bed
And my heart
Just fuelled my creativity
Some people
Can't free themselves
From the tragedy
Of where they came from
But as for me
I tend to visit
Every now and then
Just to see
If I was the reason
The flowers died
Only fools succumb
To a pedestrian life

FIERCE

A couple years ago
I saw a broken man
Stand before me
His talk still was tough
But his eyes
Weren't so fierce
And I didn't find him
To be threatening
Like he used to be
He still looked at me
Like the child I was
When I saw him last
But all I see
In front of me now
Is defeat
And tragedy
The lies
From his hands
Have forced me
To cherish the truth
In my words

THE WAR IS OVER

Bound to the hurt
Of the morphine
That smothers
Until I'm out of breath
As it stings
All the way
To California
The arrows are broken
And regrets bountiful
Your mother is gone
So is your father
And the only tie
To yesterdays
Is a son
That's so far
Out of touch
You don't exist to him
How does exile feel
When it's your turn
To crave redemption
Existing is easy now
Since all you did
Was make me bleed
The war is over
And I've turned numb

BLACKTOP

Wheels turn for miles
And the faces
Start to look the same
They get off
In unforgettable towns
With their families
Waiting for them
At the station
So happy
To see them
And the more
I see it happen
The more I wish
It would happen to me
But it never does
As I live
In a cruel exile
So I follow the sun
Where the blacktop goes

STILLBORN

Wake up screaming
From the crash
Of a straightjacket coma
Drenched in sweat
And non existent
As paper flowers
Until nerve ends deaden
Behind a torn veil
While love and hate
Shows its ugly face
And a tapestry
Of barbed wire
Thick as cancer
Soaks me in static
While the fire dies
On the edge
Of the blade
Every given moment
As if stillborn
From the mother
And father I've abhorred

UNDERPROTECTED

Throat grows hoarse
From screaming no
Eyes formerly deep sea blue
Now drenched with tears
Tried to fight back
But I'm too small
As the larger body
Crushes my tiny frame
Lips against my skin
And I feel dirty
I'd cry myself to sleep
If I could sleep at all
Daddy looks at me
Through eyes of rejection
And never comes back
So this must be my fault

STRAY

Beyond the hum
Of the air conditioner
I dance with the shrine
That enslaves
As poems
Of one night stands
Drench me
Until they live
On the page
Watching lucidity penetrate
Without grace
And I'm dangling
From the high wire
I'm the architect
Of my own destruction
But still I'm stained
Like the porcelain
Of the cup
From black coffee
No matter
How many times
I lose my breath
From the suffocation
That smothers my skin
I'll never stray
Too far from this

FEAR AND LOATHING

When you're young, grown ups can appear larger than life and for years, my stepfather Brian portrayed that image to the fullest. It was almost as if he went out of his way to fill me with the fear of him and for a long time, it worked. Whenever I would step out of line, which was a fairly often occurrence, I would be subjected a beating at his hands. And sometimes it would be more than just his hands. Being smacked with a belt was not out of the ordinary, nor was being whipped with a tree branch. As I grew older, I never truly understood instilling so much fear in me since he had to know that eventually the fear would disappear and turned into loathing. Maybe it was all about power for him, but as all dictators discover, the tide eventually turns. I'll always remember the day my version of fear came to an end. After yet another misbehaving episodes perceived by him, Brian attempted to initiate another beating, but in a plot twist that neither one of us saw coming, I just stood there poker faced. It was as if I finally had grown weary of his antics and now instead of fearing him, I just felt sorry for Brian. Once we both realized that he no longer had that grip of fear over me, the dynamic of life at home had changed and the era of loathing had begun.

SAN FRANCISCO

San Francisco
Is where I'm from
Even though
I haven't lived there
Since I was
Five years old
But it's where
I came to life
And it's where
The last time
I saw my dad
Memories of forgotten days
Flicker in and out
Of my head
Like picture postcards
Leaving me melancholy
For the cable cars
And the red bus
I used to ride
With my mother
But is no longer
In service
The day that
I was put
In a purple Ford Fairland
For the north
Was the day
That innocence died
And it would be
Thirteen years
Before I'd see home again

BRIAN

You can buy me
A bat
A glove
And a ball
But you can't
Buy me a dad
Because your idea
Of a father
Makes me choke
And when it didn't
Always go your way
It was easier for you
To just wash your hands
At the whole thing
And merely pretend
That I never existed

FATHER'S DAY

On the stoop
In front
Of the brownstone
Wearing the shirt
His father wore
Over top
Of a soul scarred
With a cut
Deeper than any knife
Could penetrate
He waits for him
To come home
Or at least
To come back
And collect
What used to be his
On Father's Day
He makes excuses
So this won't
Hit him so hard

UNVEILED

Unveiled from the whiplash
The fragility screams
Unstable to the point
Of anonymous lust
In the ruins
Of torment's temple
Edges harden
Before they should
From the devil's dance
That bleeds

Unveiled from the emotional rape
That leaves me
Feeling like an outsider
In my own skin
Somewhere between
The black wings
And this crown of thorns
I fall and inhale
The treachery
That's addicted me
In the abyss
Of drowning
I've grown stronger
Though I've also gotten colder

The skeletons
From closets of despair
Appear as ghosts
Now only dance
When I want them to
Since I've become
Unveiled and naked

BREAD AND WATER

Masks of smiles
But I'm not laughing
When the gene pool
Seems to be
Void of water
It's so easy
To be alone
In a house
Full of strangers
Masqueraded as friends
It's like trying to dance
When there is
No music playing
Or singing along
To a song
That has no words
It's gotten
To the point
That I can't tell
The difference
Between the devils
And the angels
Down to the bone
Down to nothing
But bread and water

MY TORMENT

I don't want to
Meet your new friend
I don't want to
Call him dad
Because he's not
I don't want to
Live in this broken home
I don't want to
Believe in love
I've seen the damage it does
I don't want to
Get treated like cancer
And keep getting blamed
For you being
A single parent
All my self destructive behavior
Leads back to your torment of me
So fuck you
For making I feel
Like an inconvenience
And making me feel
Like I don't matter
Fuck you for this pain
Fuck you for this life
And fuck you
For making me feel invisible
And non existent
I'll never forgive you

DADDY'S DYING

I can't tear this thorn
From my side
Until I reach the altar
And see for myself
I can't pull the weeds
Out of the earth
And see that the flowers
Are laying in regret
Until I run through
The killing fields
Where daddy's dying

NUMB

Numb to the world
I used to know
From drowning
In a godless flood
As sanity walks away
In single file
And scars turn ashen
On a razor blade tongue
The dead parade
Of useless memories
Is a twisted and callous
Cross to bear
That baptizes me
In bitter wine
While the decay
From a barbed wire mask
Scabs as I cling
To the breast
Of yesterday's tear
Maybe I've suckled
On her nipple
For too long now
How can I stare
Into the sun
When I keep falling
Between the cracks
Of the sidewalk
And when will the flood
I'm running from
Stop drowning me
Do the withered streets
Of my hometown
Consider me
The prodigal son
Or just a ghost
That's been long forgotten
As the ritual of cruelty
Begins to kiss me

Now that I'm naked
If nothing hurts
When you don't feel
I'd rather be numb

A THOUSAND MILES

Maybe its just narcissism on my part, but I've always felt a little insulted and borderline offended that there was never a custody fight over me after my parents divorced. It was as if I was the consolation prize to a marriage that ended badly. One of my only real memories I have of the man that gave me life, besides having his name, is sitting on my mother's lap somewhere between two and four years of age. My so called parents were having some sort of argument which I'm sure was about how he could pawn me off on her yet again. I do find it a little bizarre that my solitary moment of reflection is at that particular moment in time. Of course I discovered years later that I might have had another memory of him. On the day that my mother married my stepfather Brian, she spoke to my dad on the phone while I stood beside her unsuspecting who she was talking to. He didn't ask to talk to me (as far as I know, but with my mom you never know) nor did she offer the phone so I could talk to him. Though I'd known for seven or eight years now, it still stings like acid on unprotected skin. Though I don't care if I ever see him again, it will probably always bother me that he hasn't acknowledged my existence. It's been a weight that's been unbearable at times. Growing up and even now, it seems that my mother has pretended that he was never a part of her life. There were never any pictures of us as a family nor has she ever brought up his name in conversation. It's like when she married Brian, she erased the slate of her previous life. Maybe that's why we left San Francisco for British Columbia when I was five years old. We certainly couldn't take the chance of running into him and actually let me have a relationship with my father could we? Or maybe he truly just washed his hands at wanting to have a son and couldn't wait to be a thousand miles away from any reminder of me.

EDDY STREET

As I wave goodbye
To the crescents
And the waves
That cascade
Under the bridge
That connects Alameda
To the golden gates
I breathe a sigh
Under my skin
While the city lights
Fade from view

COQUITLAM

Grade school in Coquille
Filled with memories
Of far away blackboards
Finger paints
And crayon outlines
Friends I thought
Would last forever
Crystal, Laura and Michelle
The first little girls
That I kissed
But then we moved
Without a goodbye
And the next four years
Were filled with desolation
Since I seemingly
Was the only one
Who didn't know
Everyone else since birth
I couldn't wait for summer
So that I could escape
Even if it was with those
That directed me
To this prison
In the first place
The years of minimal valentines
And even more minimal friends
Would come to an end
Or so I thought
When I started high school
But that's a story
For another time

WOULD

Would the silence silhouette
The hallway outside my room
Would the shadows outside my bed
Crawl into empty spaces
Would my shelves be lined
With more than empty books
Would the cycle of numbness
Still swallow me
Would my memoir bleed off the page
Would my blue eyes
Feel like shades of grey
Would I still scream in my sleep
Would I feel so fucking incomplete
Would the pictures
That hangs in the gallery
Be more than empty frames
If he would have stayed

PHANTOMS

As the age of exile
Drags me down
Under the worms
And the decay
I'm naked in California
A million miles away
From signs of life
And the garden
In which the seeds
Were sewn in vain
While the soundtrack
Of apathy
Keeps playing endlessly
But life goes on
In this ghost town
Of a heart
Where there's plenty
Of other phantoms
To dance with
Breaking free
Of the whipping post
Until lucidity
Penetrates without grace
Nailed to the crash and burn
Of a self induced amnesia
While phantoms behind the bleeding
Martyr until a last breath

DEAD MAN'S RUIN

Dead man living
Carries the burden
Like a cancer
Of being unforgiving
As the son bleeds
And just because
He wears your name
Doesn't make you
This boy's hero
With denial of existence
Laying brutally fractured
Like a crack
In the mirror
Hate and anger
Ferments inside
And festers
Like an abscess
Blood on the highway
Blood on the hands
Of a savage heart
Without a conscience
Lungs are filled
With father's ashes
And skin is covered
With the lacerations
Of his neglect

CHRISTMAS DAY 1990

I check into
A downtown hotel
Walk into the room
Click on the light
And turn on the TV
Oblivious to the fact
That I've been left behind
Everyone I know
Is with their families
While I spend Christmas
With this bottle of wine
And even though
Its cold outside
That's nothing compared
To the chill
Inside a battered shell

SORRY

Sorry for the damage
I didn't see
And for the pain
That's locked inside
Sorry for the life
You didn't get to have
Sorry for leaving you
As the forgotten child
And for making you think
You were the reason
That your father
Walked away
Sorry was never
A word
That you said

OBSOLETE

While I watch
The ink flow
Through the needle
As it marks
My bones yet again
I bleed like distortion
From a father's scabs
Passed down
To an unsuspecting son
And damaged soaked tattoos
Remind me
What I thought
Was perfect then
Only to find out
It was make believe
And it breaks me down
Just like a needle
Breaks the skin
But even though
I'm bleeding
From the thorns
With each tattoo
You get more obsolete

FAKE FRIENDS

The night is fading
And so am I
Seem to be
Alone with my misery
This bed of nails
I lay on is freezing
The angels of mercy
Turn their backs on me
It seems that euphoria
Only comes to me
When I'm sleeping
And when I'm not breathing

It feels like I'm walking
On a razor's edge
And I can't dull the blade
No matter how hard I try
Sometimes I feel
Like I don't exist
That there's no peace
For this broken down soul

My fear of rejection
Is only eclipsed
By my fear
Of dying alone
Nothing can hurt
If you don't feel
I'm tired of the breakdowns
That fills this empty heart
This is my life
This is my destruction
I'm drowning in a sea
Of fake friends

HAPPY BIRTHDAY

Another year reminds me
What I haven't become
But this isn't a poem of self loathing
I just don't see what the big deal is
About having a birthday
What exactly is there to celebrate?
Another year older and still living?
Another year of working the assembly line?
It's not a bad job really
But I'd rather be writing words for a living
I'd rather been signing copies
Of what the masses hail
As the voice of their generation
Another year of the status quo?
I hate the status quo!
Maybe I've just become stagnant
In a life that doesn't challenge me
Maybe I just need a change
Or at least more valium
And another drink
Happy Birthday to me

BREAKING THE CHERRY OF PANDORA'S BOX OPEN

Some things
Are hard
To let go of
Like the nights
Of sleeping
In the greenhouse
With the wooden planks
As my bed
Or underneath
The bushes
In front of
My bedroom window
That you turned
Into an office
With nothing more
Than an overcoat
As my blanket
Even though time
Has painted a tapestry
Of bypass surgeries
And other
Near death incidents
I won't take my foot
Off your throat
I didn't ask to be
The bastard son
But it's a role
I can play

DEAD TO ME

The thorns of yesterday
That used to prick
Until I'd bleed
Have become dull
And not so ferocious
They've been insignificant
They've become dead to me

The demons that hollowed
Aren't so scary now
And they don't blind
The way they used to
Days of dancing
With the devil inside
Are a million miles away
They've become dead to me

I no longer
Look back in shame
The regrets don't burden me
Since I've let go
Of the talons
That cut me
Like barbed wire
It's not to say
I'm without dysfunction
But I've come to grips
With the ties
That binds me
Since the spires
That tainted
Are dead to me
Just like you Dad

DANCING INSIDE THE MOUTH OF MADNESS

Writhing on a bed
Of nails and fear
I languish alone
With this emotional crutch
While solace breathes silently
Breakable as porcelain
Under a flood of delusion
Scars forged out of cruelties
Those talons have scratched
After being torn
Out of the soil
In which I was grown
As the screams
Of the organ grind
Talk me into waging war
Against the ghosts
That torment
Like Sylvia Path
And Anne Sexton
When the blade falls
And rapture's in pieces
I find myself dancing
Inside the mouth
Of madness